CELLO

AL•LEONARD
NSTRUMENTAL
PLAY-ALONG

AUDIO
ACCESS
INCLUDED

PLAYBACK+
eed • Pitch • Balance • Loop

STAR WARS™
MUSIC FROM ALL NINE FILMS

T0057811

Audio arrangements by Peter Deneff

To access audio, visit:
www.halleonard.com/mylibrary

Enter Code
3652-3495-9615-1619

ISBN 978-1-70510-718-8

For all works contained herein:
Unauthorized copying, arranging, adapting, recording, internet posting, public performance,
or other distribution of the music in this publication is an infringement of copyright.
Infringers are liable under the law.

Visit Hal Leonard Online at
www.halleonard.com

Contact us:
Hal Leonard
7777 West Bluemound Road
Milwaukee, WI 53213
Email: info@halleonard.com

In Europe, contact:
Hal Leonard Europe Limited
42 Wigmore Street
Marylebone, London, W1U 2RN
Email: info@halleonardeurope.com

In Australia, contact:
Hal Leonard Australia Pty. Ltd.
4 Lentara Court
Cheltenham, Victoria, 3192 Australia
Email: info@halleonard.com.au

ACROSS THE STARS

(Love Theme from *"STAR WARS: ATTACK OF THE CLONES"*)

CELLO

Music by JOHN WILLIAMS

AHCH-TO ISLAND

from *STAR WARS: THE LAST JEDI*

CELLO

Music by JOHN WILLIAMS

BATTLE OF THE HEROES

from *STAR WARS: REVENGE OF THE SITH*

CELLO

By JOHN WILLIAMS

CANTINA BAND

from *STAR WARS: A NEW HOPE*

CELLO

Music by JOHN WILLIAMS

D.S. al Coda

CODA

DUEL OF THE FATES

from *STAR WARS: THE PHANTOM MENACE*

CELLO

Music by JOHN WILLIAMS

THE FOREST BATTLE

from *STAR WARS: RETURN OF THE JEDI*

CELLO

Music by JOHN WILLIAMS

HAN SOLO AND THE PRINCESS

from *STAR WARS: THE EMPIRE STRIKES BACK*

CELLO

Music by JOHN WILLIAMS

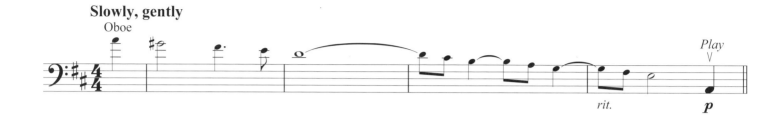

THE IMPERIAL MARCH
(Darth Vader's Theme)
from *STAR WARS: THE EMPIRE STRIKES BACK*

CELLO

Music by JOHN WILLIAMS

MARCH OF THE RESISTANCE

from *STAR WARS: THE FORCE AWAKENS*

CELLO

Music by JOHN WILLIAMS

MAY THE FORCE BE WITH YOU

from *STAR WARS: A NEW HOPE*

CELLO

Music by JOHN WILLIAMS

THE RISE OF SKYWALKER
from *STAR WARS: THE RISE OF SKYWALKER*

CELLO

Composed by JOHN WILLIAMS

PRINCESS LEIA'S THEME

from *STAR WARS: A NEW HOPE*

CELLO

Music by JOHN WILLIAMS

REY'S THEME
from *STAR WARS: THE FORCE AWAKENS*

CELLO

Music by JOHN WILLIAMS

STAR WARS
(Main Theme)
from *STAR WARS: A NEW HOPE*

CELLO

Music by JOHN WILLIAMS

THRONE ROOM *and* END TITLE

from *STAR WARS: A NEW HOPE*

CELLO

Music by JOHN WILLIAMS

YODA'S THEME

from *STAR WARS: THE EMPIRE STRIKES BACK*

CELLO

Music by JOHN WILLIAMS